How to Be Successful in Business and in Life

Discover How to Achieve Your Goals by Mastering the 7 Key Characteristics of Success

by Jonathan Mills

Table of Contents

Introduction 1

Chapter 1: Being Resilient 7

Chapter 2: Being Enthusiastic 11

Chapter 3: Being Educated 15

Chapter 4: Being Disciplined 19

Chapter 5: Being Competent 23

Chapter 6: Being Persistent 27

Chapter 7: Being Industrious 33

Conclusion 39

Introduction

While the exact meaning of success naturally differs from person to person, there are a number of universal indicators of success which cannot be disputed. Yes, you are successful at something if you have achieved a certain set of goals associated with whatever is in pursuit. However, it doesn't help if those goals are constantly changing or diluted to make up for shortcomings you uncover and accept to be a natural part of your journey.

This is especially true in the case of perhaps two of life's most important arenas: one's personal life, and the business world. It's only natural to want to live comfortably, even if your definition of comfort is simply having good health and minimizing stress. On the business front however, the definition of success ultimately comes down to one thing: profit yield. Nevertheless, even in the pursuit of financial wealth, success reveals itself to be comprised of a number of different aspects, such as the ability to have time to do things you enjoy, better health along with enough resources to maintain it, as well as recognition of some sort.

Whether you're just getting started in your quest for ultimate success or you're seeking to kick things up a notch and amass unprecedented levels of personal accomplishment; your success in business and in life depends on how you implement a specific set of seven key characteristics: You must be **Resilient, Enthusiastic, Educated, Disciplined, Competent, Persistent** and **Industrious**. That is exactly what you're going to learn in this book: How successful people utilize these seven key characteristics, and how *you* can adopt and implement these traits in *your* life too.

© Copyright 2015 by Miafn LLC - All rights reserved.

This document is geared towards providing reliable information in regards to the topic and issue covered. The publication is sold with the idea that the publisher is not required to render accounting, officially permitted, or otherwise, qualified services. If advice is necessary, legal or professional, a practiced individual in the profession should be ordered.

- From a Declaration of Principles which was accepted and approved equally by a Committee of the American Bar Association and a Committee of Publishers and Associations.

In no way is it legal to reproduce, duplicate, or transmit any part of this document in either electronic means or in printed format. Recording of this publication is strictly prohibited and any storage of this document is not allowed unless with written permission from the publisher. All rights reserved.

The information provided herein is stated to be truthful and consistent, in that any liability, in terms of inattention or otherwise, by any usage or abuse of any policies, processes, or directions contained within is solely and completely the responsibility of the recipient reader. Under no circumstances will any legal responsibility or blame be held against the publisher for any reparation, damages, or monetary loss due to the information herein, either directly or indirectly.

Respective authors own all copyrights not held by the publisher.

The information herein is offered for informational purposes solely, and is universal as so. The presentation of the information is without contract or any type of guarantee assurance.

The trademarks that are used are without any consent, and the publication of the trademark is without permission or backing by the trademark owner. All trademarks and brands within this book are for clarifying purposes only and are the owned by the owners themselves, not affiliated with this document.

Chapter 1: Being Resilient

If there is one trait that consistently and conspicuously comes up in just about all notable path-to-success stories, it is resilience. Successful people in business and in life are generally extremely resilient—they have mastered the ability to resist the abrasive effects of everything that threatens their progress, and incrementally work their way towards achieving their goals. Successful people demonstrate their resilience particularly through their dynamically built-up ability to handle criticism, not only in dismissing negative and often unwarranted criticism and ridicule, but more importantly in being able to separate negative criticism from positive, constructive criticism.

On a purely personal level, successful people are very principled and stick to their guns, NO MATTER WHAT! You can be best buddies with someone who demonstrates the right amount of resilience required to make a success out of their lives, but on the odd occasion they simply don't agree with you or what you stand for; they will never allow the fact that you are great friends shift them away from their principles. That's exactly what you have to do in order to build up your resilience; you have to determine what your goals are, clearly define your principles and ethics, map out your plan of action to achieve your goals, and then stick to your guns and implement your plan of action, NO MATTER WHAT!

Any path to success is never easy, and your resilience will be extensively tested along the way. Make no mistake—failure is anxiously waiting for the first and slightest sign of weakness; and in the absence of resilience, the difference between your success and failure is only one decisive moment of weakness. If you give up just once, it's enough to undo a lot of the work you have put in so far.

If you are ever unsure of whether the important characteristic of your resilience is receiving enough attention for its continuous development, simply go back to your original goals, go back to your original plan of action and ask yourself whether you've allowed yourself to stray. Only *you* can honestly evaluate just how much you've allowed external forces to distract you from working on achieving your goals. Life will always present you with distractions, some of which may appear to be actively working against what you aim to achieve. This is when the opportunity to build up your resilience best presents itself; because if you are able to keep working on achieving your goals when it's particularly difficult, when the storm inevitably dies down, you can come back much stronger and get some serious momentum going.

Successful people demonstrate their resilience through their dedication to making progress every day, even if that progress is marginal. If you want to be successful, you'll have to dedicate a portion of your daily life to making progress, regardless of how short on time you think you are, how many millions of other things you have to do, or how much negative criticism you appear to be getting.

Don't lose sight of your goals, stick to your principles and always make a conscious effort to get right back to your plan of action, and you'll very quickly build up the type of resilience required to make a success out of your life and business endeavors. Resilience entails the ability to always find your way back to the basics and adapt to any external forces without losing sight of what you originally set out to achieve—a key ingredient for success in life and in business.

Chapter 2: Being Enthusiastic

Enthusiasm is another very important ingredient successful people always add to their breakfast smoothies. They live, eat and breathe their business and make whatever it is they've dedicated their lives to the main part of their daily lives.

Now there's only one way to ensure you're enthusiastic about what you've chosen to do, with the ultimate aim of achieving success, and that is simply doing something you love doing. If you are not passionate about anything you do, you can forget about maintaining the amount of enthusiasm required to keep the fire burning in order for you to achieve your goals.

In the specific case of business, if your line of business is centered on something you're not even remotely interested in, you just have to institute some wholesale changes. There is simply no other way—otherwise at some point, questions of exactly "why you're doing this" will overwhelm your desire to keep working on meeting your ongoing objectives. It's hard enough staying focused on something you truly love doing, even a hobby, so you have to pursue something you have a passion for in order to remain enthusiastic.

Enthusiasm as a required trait for success may come across as a bit cliché, especially since most people find it quite difficult to formulate a link between doing something they love and earning money. While the saying "follow your passion and the money will come" isn't always a practical phrase to live by, developing a passion for something doesn't necessarily entail selecting something you'd do even if you weren't getting paid for it. It's never as cut and dry as starting a business selling something you've always been interested in making or offering a service related to something that's second nature to you. Passion develops from discovering that you're extremely good at something, to the extent that you get more recognition than would be deemed normal.

So in order to remain enthusiastic about what you're pursuing and maintain your success trajectory, pursue something you have a natural flair for or something you've become particularly good at and actually enjoy doing.

Chapter 3: Being Educated

Successful people are educated, and the extent to which they are educated gives them a set of deployable skills that come together with a powerful knowledgebase to account for the ability to spot opportunities and successfully capitalize on each of those opportunities. An educated mind is also equipped with the necessary skills to adapt to each situation and very quickly iterate through all the possibilities to ultimately give you the best chance at edging closer to success.

It's safe to say that education is a very important part of what breeds success, but by no means does it suggest that formal, academic education is the be all and end all of success in business and in life. Think about it—some of the wealthiest and most successful people don't necessarily hold Master's degrees. If anything, by the time they are done with their formal academic education, they usually discover that the path they've embarked on does not necessarily represent something they're truly passionate about.

A formal education is great and can do wonders for your chances at success, but there are so many different ways through which you can educate yourself. People who go on to make successes out of their lives and their business endeavors see every single day and every single experience as a brand new opportunity to learn something new. When it comes to working your way towards success, every little thing matters. Absolutely everything matters—from the way you conduct your research, right up to how you manage your time, interact with people and even package and deliver your unique offering. Education is also what ensures you actually have something of value to offer, paving the way for your success.

In this day and age of the wired (or wireless) world, educating yourself starts with a simple Internet search. Previously, some very expensive info-gathering tasks required undertakings such as making appointments with attorneys, visiting the title deeds office or going through the large bibliography of your local library, stockpiled with a collection of books that are probably outdated. Nowadays, you don't even need to speak to an attorney and get charged by the hour to learn about the legalities surrounding any of your endeavors. You can pretty much acquire any technical skills through the knowledge you accumulate online.

If you want to emulate the success of those who've done it before you, one of the keys to your success is education. Get educated by taking every new opportunity to expand your knowledgebase. Attend masterminds if you can, but what you must absolutely do is connect and network with like-minded people. It's much easier to grasp something when it comes from someone who shares a common interest and preferably someone who has done what you intend to do.

At the end of every day or whenever you have an opportunity to reflect on the designated period that was, jot down a quick summary of what you've learned. You can use keywords or cue phrases as long as you have something you can always go back to and perhaps digest much better since your mind won't always be in the right frame to retain new information.

Successful people are constantly investing in themselves and their education, and that's what you should get into the habit of doing too. Your mind is your greatest asset and nobody can ever take what you've learned away from you.

Chapter 4: Being Disciplined

This is another one of those characteristics successful people not only preach openly, but are also clearly depicted to practice consistently. You definitely have to be disciplined in order to succeed at anything, particularly in business and life in general.

This is when it gets real though, because being disciplined is in no way easy. Discipline simply means staying focused on chipping away at the identified tasks you need to complete in order to eventually realize your goals and achieve success. At its core, discipline entails the acknowledgment of all the distractions and even all the different opportunities that may come your way while you're on your path to achieving your goals, but you have to be able to focus your attention on what's most important to you. Discipline is exercised very simply by making a choice between what you want right now as temporary pleasure or comfort and what you ultimately want to achieve in your business and in life.

There will be times when you don't really feel like working on your personal development or on your business. There's absolutely no problem with taking a breather now and then, but the inner big brother in you has to be sensible and call you back to order.

Exercising discipline and self-control is a process mastered through continuous practice. What you need to understand is that there is no such thing as perfection as far as discipline and self-control goes. Whenever you inevitably wander off the path to achieving your goals and you don't quite put in the work you know you're supposed to, get back on track, forgive yourself and make up for it by renewing your commitment to your pursuit of success.

The key to remaining disciplined resides in a combination of a number of sub-habits you should adopt, including the creation of a schedule or setting aside some time each day to work on accomplishing certain goals, ridding your immediate surroundings of all distractions and temptations, working on your health to maintain good energy levels and rewarding yourself for achieving predetermined milestones.

Remember not to be too hard on yourself during moments of weakness, but be sure to compensate for any moments of breaking your discipline by putting in even more effort when you get back to your grind.

Chapter 5: Being Competent

Competence is one of those key characteristics of successful people that go without saying, but one which has to be mentioned nonetheless. It is a bare minimum and you simply cannot do without being competent if you want to survive, let alone get ahead and become successful.

Successful people understand that there is no room for incompetence, especially in the business world; and being competent means that you always deliver on your mandate and simply do what needs to be done. As someone who is competent, you have to refrain from making any excuses and ensuring never to put yourself in a position that requires you to make up excuses. Whether the obligation is to you or to someone else, if you find yourself having to think up excuses, you need to work on your competence.

In order to ensure you remain competent, you have to develop the ability to think on your feet and also develop your ability to implement damage control. When working on your personal and business development, you don't get rewarded for effort. Your goals and your success don't materialize simply because of the effort you put in, but rather materialize as a result of meeting certain deliverables. You don't get paid or rewarded for completing 99.9% of the job—you get paid and rewarded for completing 100% of the job.

Another important factor required for you to remain competent is the varied amounts of effort you'll have to put in, in order to get the job done and meet specific goals. There are times when you might literally have to run just to stand still and keep up with the trends to stay relevant in the market. The same applies to your personal success—your dynamic domestic life will at times require you to become a whole lot more involved just to stay up to speed.

To ensure you remain competent in everything you do while working towards your success and achieving your goals, you have to invariably commit to fulfilling your key commitments. Whatever it is you're pursuing, it will very quickly become apparent to you what is of utmost importance to maintain your progress. You know what needs to be done so get it done, no matter how many other added challenges you might have to contend with.

Competent people, who become successful as a result, don't make up excuses but always ensure, at the very least, to deliver what is expected of them—something which should very quickly become second nature to you if you want to be successful too. Always honor your word and you'll instantly give off the impression of someone who is competent, while actually working on your competence in the abovementioned ways.

Chapter 6: Being Persistent

Persistence is another one of those traits which are synonymous with successful people. Ask anyone who is successful in business and in life what the one thing they mostly attribute their success to and, nine-out-of-ten times, they'll tell you a story of how they simply refused to give up. Persistence definitely does pay off, but it is definitely not an easy trait to adopt and consistently deploy.

If attaining success were easy, the thick skin required for you to exercise persistence would be so common that it wouldn't even be an issue worthy of discussion. Persistent people realize how much of a necessity it is to challenge the status quo and explore those corners others are either too afraid to challenge or are bound by the various pigeonholes into which society expects them to fit.

The idea of being persistent is undoubtedly a very positive one and it's conceptually very simple. In practice however, it is NOT easy to insist on pursuing something when its intended yield is very difficult to spot even in the distance. It appears to be human nature for all of us to want to find a place to belong to, especially when the various common pigeonholes from which you are encouraged to choose are constantly reinforced and bandied about in your face. Wherever you go and whatever you do in life, you are constantly required to group or class yourself to fall into a specific predetermined profile. This constant profiling is one of the biggest killers of momentum and persistence, so it's something you'll have to learn to look beyond if you want to be successful, particularly in the business world.

Successful people typically pride themselves on what makes them unique, and the biggest and best success stories are themed on people whose persistence challenged a lot of conventions along the way. If someone says to you "you can't do that" or something like "that's not within convention," ask why. This is when the value of being persistent is often misinterpreted and misdirected because there is a difference between persisting with something that merely fulfills a routine and persisting with something that incrementally moves you closer to meeting targets and ultimately achieving success.

There is a popular story commonly told among some of the world's most popular motivational circles, and it speaks of one of the most common starting points of people seeking to get into business, take control of their own lives and succeed financially and otherwise. Door-to-door sales—the story depicts the attitude adopted by two sales people who happen to be good friends. One of them proclaims to simply not be able to handle getting doors repeatedly slammed in his face, quite rudely too, by the uninterested prospective clients. This particular sales person inevitably proceeded to give up door-to-door sales and returned to the nine-to-five rat race he'd been meaning to escape.

His friend on the other hand took a different view and decided that he would persist until he succeeded one way or the other. Salesman number two learnt that there is an average door-to-door sales conversion rate of around 12% for the television sets they were selling, and so he realized that in order to succeed, he simply had to persist and knock on 100 doors for every 12 sales he wanted to make.

If you want to be successful, you have to adopt the second person's philosophy —reduce whatever it is you're pursuing to a numbers game and persist until you start to see some results. This is the type of persistence you need to effect—the type of persistence that yields progress, as opposed to persisting with something that yields the same amount of output each and every time.

Learn to revel in the experience of getting "doors slammed in your face" because with each door that gets slammed in your face, you're one door closer to your next sale. So what if "the crowd" operating under the spell of their herd-mentality thinks you're crazy or would be embarrassed to do what you're doing? Their approval or disapproval of you won't help you achieve your goals and become successful. Their approval of you will only cause you to become average (like them), when what you need to do is become motivated by your fear of being average. People who persistently follow the crowd remain average, while those who persistently seek to explore new territory will inevitably uncover their ticket to the big time.

You have to be motivated by the prospect of your success, persistently working on breaking new ground and incrementally making progress. The previous chapter covered competence as one of the seven key traits synonymous with successful people, with the commitment to honoring your word forming part of what makes you competent. As part of what it requires to be persistent in order to work your way to success, you have to flip the script on competence. You need to expect and demand competence from people you network and connect with, particularly those whom you enter into agreements with. In the same way you're going to commit to being competent (and honoring your word), be persistent in collecting your dues from those who have made a commitment to you. Bug them until they deliver—they are the ones who have something to be embarrassed about and not you. This is the type of persistence required for you to ultimately succeed in business and life, and this is the type of persistence successful people live by.

Chapter 7: Being Industrious

Last but definitely not least is good old-fashioned hard work. Successful people don't even have to admit this as a key trait for success and there simply is no substitute for hard work. You have to be industrious in order to achieve success.

In the business world specifically, one of the major barriers to entry and ultimately to success is just how much hard work has to be put in. Most people fall off along the way as a direct result of not working hard enough on whatever they want to achieve. Successful people on the other hand work harder than anybody else they know, but there is one thing they season their relentless industry with—something which many of them may not even realize, and that is the ability to apply the multiplier effect and duplicate their industriousness.

Successful people work incredibly hard, but they work very smartly too. On whatever side of the fence you find yourself (whether you're working for yourself or if you're employed), you will constantly hear the need for you to be industrious and put in hard work. Hard work and industry becomes smart work and strategic industriousness when you know exactly where to direct your greatest efforts. Again, if your hard work takes the form of a routine, which in turn yields the same output after each cycle, you need to rethink your approach and try to find ways to redirect your industry to something that incrementally produces progression.

The story of two gold prospectors comes to mind in an attempt to demonstrate hard grinding and industry versus smart grinding and strategic industriousness. The story features two gold prospectors who have both come across some accurate information about a piece of public domain land rich in gold, just waiting to be collected by those willing to make the trip. In this scenario, the hard-working prospector would wake up each day with his shovel and wheelbarrow in tow to dig up the gold and sell it for profit. This prospector's yield would then be directly proportional to the amount of hard work he puts in and granted; depending on how hard he works, he can make some great profits.

Truly successful people however aren't merely satisfied with the opportunity to output yields that are directly proportional to their industriousness. Successful people take the form of the second gold prospector, who decided he is definitely going to go and dig up some gold himself, but he is also going to recruit other gold prospectors, sell them the information he has about the location of the gold-rich vein and for good measure, sell each of them a wheelbarrow and a shovel.

If you want to be successful in business and in life, you have to be the second gold prospector and look for ways to "exist" in more than one place at a time, applying some serious industry to each of those realms in which you co-exist.

To bring this analogy more in line with modern times, business success is the reserve of those who have mastered the art of working hard ON their business as opposed to working hard IN their business. The comparison between a lifestyle entrepreneur and a growth entrepreneur comes to mind. A lifestyle entrepreneur is merely someone who works for themselves and has perhaps set up a business, but is still selling his own skills and time in order to make money. A growth entrepreneur on the other hand typically works hard on growing his business and perhaps on getting more clients and instituting systems that collectively work hard for the growth and progression of his business.

Successful people definitely work very hard and are industrious in that way, but their hard work and industry is strategically deployed to processes which won't require their direct involvement ever. You can learn to easily identify the right places to pour your industry by simply taking a step back and looking at the bigger picture of each task you occupy yourself with. Is there perhaps a direct route to the client you could explore and could you delegate a number of the key tasks that take up most of your time?

Once you've learned how to strategically deploy your industriousness, you'll be well on your way to fast-tracking your success, but remember that the key word is industry. You simply have to put in the hard work, one way or the other.

Conclusion

The difference between average people and those people who are successful in business and in life resides in 7 key traits possessed, developed and consistently implemented. Success in business is very closely related to personal success and life in general, so the same key characteristics successful business people implement in their businesses are deployed in their personal lives.

If you are to succeed in business and in life, you have to be:

Re**S**ilient

Enth**U**siastic

Edu**C**ated

Dis**C**iplined

Comp**E**tent

PersiStent

InduStrious

As will increasingly become apparent to you, all seven key traits depicted by those who are successful in business and in life are interlinked. You cannot choose one trait and run with it without adopting ALL the others at the same time. Resilience, Enthusiasm, Education, Discipline, Competence, Persistence, and Industriousness all come together to account for success and you have to constantly work on developing all these traits if you want to succeed in your business and life.

Resilience is developed through your ability to make sure you always return to what needs to be done and what matters most, despite all the forces acting against what you might be working on. Enthusiasm is very important because it is what will keep you going and keep you chipping away at the tasks mapped out, which will eventually lead to your success. To maintain enthusiasm about your daily tasks on your path to success, you simply have to pursue something for which you have a passion.

Take every opportunity to educate yourself so that you are adequately skilled to handle everything that needs to be done and also so that you are able to spot opportunities as they dynamically reveal themselves to you as you go along. Successful people constantly invest in their personal development through their education, but this doesn't always mean you have to go the formal, academic route to acquire new and useful skills and valuable information. Conduct frequent research, network and connect with like-minded people and people who have set a precedent for you. Attend focus groups, mastermind and training seminars to continuously educate yourself in various ways.

Remaining disciplined to increase your chances of success and to fast track your path to success entails ridding your immediate surroundings of distractions and always finding a way to get back to work when distractions inevitably get one over you.

Competence goes hand-in-hand with educating yourself and simply making sure you at least get what's expected of you done according to acceptable standards. Competence ensures basic survival, providing a solid base to go the extra mile; set yourself apart from the norm and get ahead like all successful people do.

Finally, successful people very effectively bring persistence together with industriousness. If you persistently work very hard on strategic developmental processes within your life and your business, it will inevitably pay off and you are almost guaranteed the success you desire.

Finally, I'd like to thank you for purchasing this book! If you enjoyed it or found it helpful, I'd greatly appreciate it if you'd take a moment to leave a review on Amazon. Thank you!